SELLING IS JOY

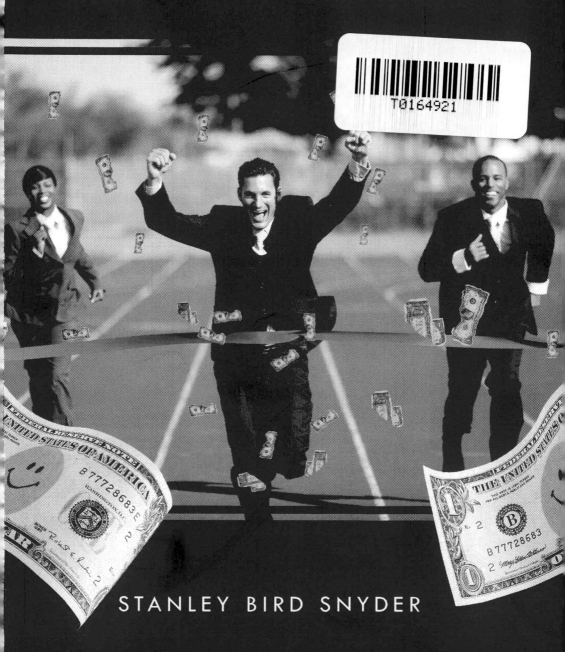

STANLEY BIRD SNYDER

Selling is Joy

Selling is Joy

Stanley Bird Snyder

Order this book online at www.trafford.com
or email orders@trafford.com

Most Trafford titles are also available at major online book retailers.

Printed in the United States of America.

ISBN: 978-1-4269-9339-8 (sc)
ISBN: 978-1-4269-9340-4 (e)

Library of Congress Control Number: 2011915426

Trafford rev. 09/06/2011

 www.trafford.com

North America & international
toll-free: 1 888 232 4444 (USA & Canada)
phone: 250 383 6864 ♦ fax: 812 355 4082

To Ed Bachorik

Ed Bachorik, my friend and mentor, worked with me for fifteen years. He remained my friend until he passed away in 1981 at age sixty-one. His wife, Julia, said that the last person he wrote to before he died was me, and I treasure that letter. Ed rose through the ranks from sales correspondent to executive vice president of the Allied Control Company Inc. Ed challenged and encouraged me to do good things beyond what seemed possible for me to accomplish. This writing depicts a journey that I made through the years in successful selling and marketing. Ed was the first to encourage me in this great undertaking.

Contents

Preface

This story is an accounting of the highlights in my sales and marketing experience. It is hoped that you may gain some knowledge, insight, wisdom, and maybe inspiration from it.

Requirements of successful selling are the following: a passion to sell; the ability to work with all kinds of people, to become a servant, and to be a self-starter; good discipline; good communication skills; patience; and the desire to share in the customer's success. If your makeup, experience, and education support these attributes, you are qualified to practice the art of the selling profession. It can be a continued practice toward perfection, or toward what you may consider success. You should have joy while practicing!

Come with Me

So you still want to sell? It is a misunderstood profession. People can see what other professionals or workers do, but if you are a true salesperson, they oftentimes think that you just take orders. People think that you drive around in a new car, probably to a golfing appointment. The real truth eludes them. Just being an order taker requires obedience, accuracy, and little else.

We're looking at people who identify the market, seek out a customer, penetrate the account to learn who makes the decisions, and then identify their need so you can develop interest in your product, seek out known quantities to be quoted for a sale, keep working to develop approval, produce a competitive offer, close the order, and follow up with customer service. With a key account this can take months before the business is placed. However, the rewards are great. If your main goal is to make money quickly, you may be disappointed. If your goal is satisfaction of what you can accomplish with great joy, you have the best goal in mind. Money rewards will follow. All of this is called "response capability."

What Market?

The discussion here is about the OEM (original equipment manufacturer) market, or the companies that use and purchase components to use in their systems. Most of my experience has been selling components to major systems manufacturers. A key account is a systems manufacturer that uses large numbers of the product or component that you hope to sell to them. These key accounts are chosen as your target for focus to manage a strong selling campaign. Hopefully one can attain a composite wisdom in selling from this journey.

My early experience has been with manufacturer's marketing, both inside and in the field as a direct representative, and later as an independent sales rep. That became my greatest challenge in starting my own sales rep business. It seemed I would need to walk on water. However, my wife Judy and good friends encouraged me to trust and go.

Nothing Happens until Something Is Sold

Selling oftentimes goes two ways. Upon a special need, you must work with your own factory to learn all about their strongest capabilities to bring about a mutually profitable deal. Actually, you need to be in-depth at the customer's location and at the company you are representing. You must fully understand the needs and ability or requirements of both to translate need into a sale. Managing the capability into a sale could be called "a marriage business style."

Personality is an attribute, because you want people to like you. Think about this. Two people leave the same school with the same education. One can't wait to be a buyer; the other has a passion to sell. What a difference! How come? The buyer's personality is to be in control with definite parameters. He likes to work within structure. On the other hand, the good salesman is a loner, a dreamer, plays options, dislikes controlling others, and has a servant attitude. The salesman on average has the opportunity to make more pay or commission, and he has much more freedom. A good salesman actually sets his own pay scale by intelligently pursuing probable business from as many accounts as he can find. In essence, he can control his own destiny! He manages his own time. Both buyers and salesmen are needed as extremely valuable to business. Together they should form a good bridge between supply and need. It's the passion that drives us both. I could not do his job well at all, and most likely he would go nuts trying to do mine. Buyers have said that to me. A buyer friend said, "I don't know how you stand that kind of abuse." Because the reward is great and fulfilling, that's why! We in the field of selling need to build and to be a good bridge to the customer and back to our supplier. It's a two-way information highway.

Sometimes reckless abandon or personal risk is required to sell major potentials. Come along on this wonderful journey and be surprised, laugh a little, and understand our world of selling a little better.

Starting Early

My first sales effort started at age eleven. I contracted to sell the *Saturday Evening Post* and *Life* magazines door to door. They were delivered by me, monies were collected, and I would pick them up from the distributors at an agreed-upon location. Going house to house to establish a base of customers and then delivering the magazines on a spread-out basis was tough work. I thought about it. In a nearby area was a group of high-rise apartment buildings concentrated in a six-block area. Selling and delivering there was much more efficient since the elevators did the traveling. Many were sold there, delivered, and monies collected. I made a fair wage, I thought.

As a side benefit on those deliveries, over time I collected tons of newspapers and magazines from the same area for the Boy Scout World War II effort.

After the war, with the advent of television, there arose a need that offered sales potential. TV screens were very small, so many people wanted to buy magnifiers to place over the small screens. The models I sold were made of plastic, which was polarized to enlarge the picture with an easy installation. Many were sold, so I was very pleased.

Taking Care of Business

My very first full-time employment started in 1948 at Ward Leonard Electric Company in Mount Vernon, New York. As an office boy, I delivered mail all around the many factory locations in town. On these trips, I could visit manufacturing, the toolroom, the plating facility, the laboratory, shipping, receiving, engineering, and the general office. Most of my time was in the sales department doing paperwork. My area was near the corporate offices of the chairman, president, executive vice president, and all of the sales and administrative managers. The remaining staff officers were located in their respective departments.

Special mention is made here of George Camp, the sales manager emeritus. George was most important to the company because of his can-do attitude of helpfulness. He knew our customers well, and they often sought his advice. He taught me about selling, and he was first to open the mail containing orders. He looked them over before giving them to sales. It was his practice to review the commission checks going out to their reps. On occasion he would call to congratulate them on their tangible success. His idea of being involved showed wisdom only gained through a lot of practice. Camp's ideas were used by me many years later. George, at eighty plus, died with his boots on while I was working there. He was greatly missed, but his congenial manner stayed with me. During my time there, I decided that I wanted to be a company salesman. Our men were well dressed, congenial, drove new cars, and wore Stetson hats with a red feather! These guys were enthusiastic and had a passion for their work.

It Pays to Have Good Friends

In 1952 a corporate buyer at Western Electric in New York City, whom I served while working at Ward Leonard, told me that Allied Control Company in New York City was looking for an inside salesperson to handle their account. I was interested, so they called Allied and set up an appointment for me. I was hired immediately and continued working with my friend Tony Pina, a purchasing agent at AT&T. My new position gave me overall responsibility for servicing all of the AT&T, Western Electric, and Bell Laboratories accounts. Allied was a leader in miniature, high-reliability relay design and manufacturing. It pays to have good friends, especially in high places!

A Tenuous Situation and Hymns

At Allied, our orders for relays to be installed in the Nike missile guidance system by Western Electric were becoming overdue and were of great concern to everyone, especially the procurement people from the North Carolina Works Factory. Three of their procurement managers came to our New York City office to expedite these late deliveries and to ensure that their critical need was satisfied. After meetings with our CEO, they were still skeptical. My boss, Ed Bachorik, offered to take them and me to our factory in Plantsville, Connecticut, where they could see what efforts were under way to meet their schedules. The trip up in Ed's car seemed long because these men were not conversant or cordial. At the plant, after a tour of the production facility, we all met with the plant manager. He offered his personal management to expedite the needed deliveries.

The six of us pilgrims started on our way back in Ed's auto. These high-level men could not be placated without positive results that they hoped were forthcoming quickly.

Rolling along the scenic Connecticut countryside it all seemed so peaceful, yet these men did not seem to enjoy their ride. To lighten up the gloomy atmosphere within that auto, I started to hum to myself a well-known hymn. Immediately their leader picked it up and sang the words. Then we all chimed in together. For an hour we sang Christian hymns, to the delight of everyone. It seemed that we had Baptist, Catholic, Methodist, and Lutheran singers, who turned the gloom into Sonshine!

Being all brothers, this family of positive attitudes produced good result, and we continued selling to Western Electric. When all seems gloomy, sing a hymn!

We met our schedules well on time. I used that good news to learn from them about forthcoming new business. In the future they called me to help by giving them up-to-date information on their business.

A Yankee Goes South

It was necessary to go to Western Electric in Winston-Salem with a list six feet long of their order status that the buyer Clyde Dula had requested. These orders were so important to them that they needed personal management on my part, so down I went. Being my first trip into the South, I was concerned, not knowing what to expect. The meetings in their conference room were attended by several white-haired senior managers, and in their midst I felt a little inadequate. At one point I even felt a little threatened by these powerful men. At that point Clyde Dula stood up and said something like this: "We consider ourselves southern gentlemen, so please don't give our friend Stan a hard time. We asked him to come down to help, and I believe he will." Encouraged by Clyde, we went on to better understand each other's needs.

Clyde took me to dinner, and we had a nice evening together. He asked me to stay over and go to church with him on Sunday, which I did. From that time on, I considered Clyde as my southern brother. As I wrote this, I called Clyde in his home, and he was pleased that I remembered him. He is now eighty-nine years old and in reasonably good health. He said that he was still selling a few parts to local companies. Clyde left purchasing in the '60s and has continued ever since. He is one of the few buyers that successfully went out to sell.

Terrible News!

Everything seemed to be going well, so why insert bad news here? Hopefully there is a human side to business, and this happening should be used as a eulogy for Ed Bachorik.

Ed noticed my downcast look and asked what was bugging me. I blurted out that my seven-year-old son, Roy, was diagnosed with terminal cancer, and there was little hope. Ed took me into his office and called the hospital where Roy was to see if there was anything that he could do to help. After getting all the information he could, Ed then ordered me to leave the office every day at 2:00 p.m. to be able to visit Roy in the hospital. For three months this went on, and each day Ed would ask what I needed.

At Roy's funeral, Ed made sure that almost everyone in the office attended. The church was overflowing. Afterward, outside, Ed said, "Do you suppose that you could do a little work for a change?"

"Sure, I'll be in tomorrow."

"No, you won't. Take the rest of the week and get lost. See ya Monday."

The following week at work, Ed called me in and asked me to gather up all the hospital bills and give them to our chief accountant to review them. He said, "They're all crooks, and I don't want them to cheat you."

So I did and never saw the bills again! When I asked about those hospital bills, he said, "Stop bothering me; so we won't advertise for a month. Don't get soft on me Snyder—get to work!" For Ed, I would go into the fire. At least, I would do my very best for him, and as you read on you will see that I did—and even entered the fire at times!

Big City—Small Church

What has this got to do with selling? The very most, you will see! During Roy's funeral, two buses chugged away outside of the church. With open windows in the August heat, the noise and smoke from buses running outside was very annoying. It was their turnaround stop, and even the church, including our bishop, could not get it removed. I was so incensed about it that I was determined to do something. But what? I couldn't fight the City of New York. It is written that "faith of a mustard seed can move a mountain," so I got one moved!

The chairman of Allied Control, C. L. VonEgloffstein, was in our office one day, and I asked him if we could talk. After listening to my plight about the church and buses, he said, "Leave it with me." So I did.

In a few days, the bus stop was removed, the sidewalk was repaved, asphalt was replaced, and the turnaround was installed across the wide boulevard next to Van Courtland Park! There the city workers installed a wall into the bank of the park, which was large and attractive. That spot is known as "Roy's turnaround." Beside myself with gratitude for what Von had done, he smiled and said, "It's nothing. Mayor Wagner and I are fraternity brothers. So I told him it was wrong for the city to pick on a church. It was done, and the whole episode around Roy had matured me greatly.

I was truly empowered to do great things, within my capability, for my company! That is a powerful motivation.

Hands across the Border

A creative idea from Ed Bachorik was to periodically hold a dinner meeting of key personnel from both locations of the company, at a restaurant halfway between New York City and the Plantsville, Connecticut, factory. Good relations were fostered among the different disciplines of effort. Sales always felt that the factory acted in self-interest because they were removed from any customer exposure. Consequently, sales set up programs that were unrealistic to the manufacturing location. In many cases the factory could better serve the customer if involved with the plans early on. Having now established good friendships, we apprised the factory on how best to offer a good business plan to our customers. There is nothing like getting everyone involved. It does, however, require good judgment from sales management, and Ed had the ability to do.

As a side benefit, Ed provided entertainment to be enjoyed by all at these meetings with the factory people. Before one meeting, Ed was busy collecting what he considered to be interesting pictures to be shown on a screen during an upcoming meeting. To those of us who knew the characters represented by the pictures, it was hilarious but also pointed. A picture of Rip Van Winkle in his gray beard was said to be a picture of our customer awaiting delivery. Another was a horse-drawn cart, said to be our expedited delivery method. The third was a shark, said to be our credit manager. A man standing on the edge of a half-completed bridge while gazing at the other half, which did not meet, was our chief engineer. The picture of Fort Knox was said to be the estate of our chairman of the board of directors, VonEglofstein. Our final inspection department was depicted by a cart dumping refuse at a garbage dump. The final one, an Adirondack Mountain bear pawing amid a garbage dump, brought the house down. It was said to be our Western Electric inspector at work in our plant! Read on about Western Electric.

One Step Back, and Then Way Forward

Being in charge of servicing our largest account, Western Electric, I was called by their North Carolina factory buyer and told that our product was failing in the guidance system of the Nike missile being built there. The failures, confirmed as being the fault of our relays, caused line stopping in the customer's factory and were a threat to national security. This news hit the industry like stuff hitting the proverbial fan. Bad news travels fast and wide! We assembled our leading design, QA, production, and engineering people to fly down to their plant. Our tails were between our legs on this most serious complaint. Assembled in the meeting, chaired by the director of Bell Telephone Laboratory, Charles Schneider, we were told all about this tragic series of failures. A small group of our people entered the restricted secret manufacturing area. An hour later they all returned with heads bowed as if in prayer. Schneider announced that the Western Electric factory people had mishandled our units by faulty methods of installation. Thousands of failed product were in operating equipment not yet shipped out. The four present hymn singers then smiled at us as if to say mmmmmming!

My people breathed a deep sigh of relief and left the plant respectfully. I remained with Schneider to see how best we could help them recover. We instituted an absolute high-priority recovery program, to the satisfaction of all.

When I reported this recovery schedule to the director of procurement, I asked him how we could recover from such negative, widely spread news, since the good news for us would only be a whimper. This director said to me that with our very high performance rating, he would personally see that we received special consideration on any future business. To me, this extracted promise was good partnering! To my knowledge, we never lost a major contract over the years I worked there! Allied Control was considered to be the best in its field by all of the Bell System people.

Over the years we had the privilege of dealing with some wonderful people at Western Electric in North Carolina. People like C. W. Zartman, works manager; Bill Cooker and Dave Henise, procurement managers; and Clyde Dula, Connor Fanelty, Phil Brooks, Joe Waters, Doc Kinsinger, and Archie Brown were all friends and in procurement management. How a company responds to a customer complaint can determine its success as a supplier in the future. It can assure your customer that you are committed to making things right. It offers an opportunity to prove its good recovery capability. In this instance we gained a great reputation with our largest account. It was a lesson to be remembered. Again, it is, "response capability."

The Buck Didn't Stop Here

Our contracts with Western Electric were as a subcontractor and were subject to government ASPR clauses. One regulation allowed us 12 percent gross profit on the contracts for relays. If we went over the 12 percent, we could request retaining the overage to be used in R&D, which would eventually benefit the government. No such luck on this go-around, where the overage in profit was large. Ed Bachorik, in his wisdom, decided to present the overage back to the buyer. He got a check drawn for $30,000, and with it we went down to Western Electric, where he presented it with great fanfare to the buyer. Ed had the local press take pictures and include a write-up, to be widely published throughout the Western Electric locations. It got us not only good press but was supportive to all of those that we dealt with. On Ed's part, this was a stroke of genius, and I was very proud to be a part of it.

Smokestack Selling

In early America, manufacturing plants sprang up along rivers and streams. They utilized the moving water to turn paddles, which in turn moved the wheels of machinery inside the adjacent factories.

Later, many of these river-located plants changed over to steam power since it offered greater flexibility. Marketing intelligence was still hit-or-miss, mostly miss. Massachusetts, Connecticut, and New York led the industrial revolution because of a number of factors. One was a demographic makeup of skilled workers. In this population were buyers of these products. What about the lonely salesman? How did he ferret out those factories that needed to purchase parts? Imagine this; there were no highways and few railroads to get around. He traveled by horseback over hill and dale. Coming over the brow of a hill, he could view the valley and hillsides ahead to see smoking chimneys. Aha, there's production going on over there. Let's go see. Carrying his literature and samples in, he sees that they make clocks there. So he can sell wood for the cases, spring material for escapement, screws, etc. Finding those places by rote then was called "smokestack selling." These pioneer sales guys were a rugged lot and sold whatever would sell, oftentimes taking the risk to buy the item and then resell it for immediate delivery at a much greater profit margin. Thus was the birth of distributors, another level of selling. Salesmen earned 5 percent to 10 percent commission on products sold and paid for.

Distributor Markets

Commodity items such as standard sizes of screws, nuts, bolts, washers, and clamps were needed quickly for assembling a product. As with lightbulbs, there are common parts that can be purchased from a distributor. He bought these in volume at a low wholesale price. These were then sold in small volume at retail price, thus the markup profit. To be effective, they carried stock of often-used parts in a horse-driven wagon. Larger, heavier loads were driven by two horses. Unlike a product salesman, they sold anyone's product—whichever gave them the greatest profit margin. There was little loyalty to a certain product manufacturer since they owned the product at the selling point. The risk was his to sell his inventory at a turnover at least four times a year. For many years the "Smokestack Selling" method persisted. The market targeted by us is known as OEM, original equipment manufacturing." The various levels of markets are: raw material, components, OEM, subassemblies, test systems power supplies, and end product or system. In today's market, distributors don't seem to function as they should. Their salespeople see a large quantity buy coming up for a product from one of their suppliers. Working under a policy agreement, they are not tightly bound to sell exclusively for one manufacturer; thus we could lose an order for standard products. It also does not give the buyer the best price because the disty guy is buying in the same quantity as the buyer but then adds his price to the quote. In other words, he got in between us and really did not perform his function as taking a risk of large buy of standards to markup price to sell in small quantities. In some cases, a customer preferred buying from a certain distributor, and that is their call.

New Product Ideas

One thing is sure, "All new ideas and products come from the field or customers." They're the ones with the pressing need: "If you could only supply a unit with this and that to perform as required at a good price, we will buy millions of them." Now, given the details of the customer's wish list, the guys in the back room go to work. They're called R&D, research and development engineering. They were guided by the need of the market via salespeople. If they were the input for new ideas, we would be trying to sell the ultimate lightbulb, which could not fit anyone's socket. My company tried that route once and wound up destroying $200,000 worth of tools to have been used in trying to manufacture a unique, fail-safe product. Eventually sales could not sell this black sheep, which could not fit anyone's connecter or interface. Engineering prevailed because they sold the decision makers on the merits of their design. So much for the crystal ball! Eighty percent of all new products come from the field. You will see the 80/20 law used in many areas of marketing and business. Later we will show what creative selling is, and how we can create a market; which is extremely rare.

Send in the Bloodhounds

The sad conclusion to this segment is awakening. "Eighty percent
new products fail." Wow! How can that be? First, we aren't aware of
failures, probably because they're not ours. It's a whole new research
to study why they failed. Any of the following could have been the c
lack of proper funding, wrong design target, market shift, no penetr
at user accounts, a lack of experienced sales staff, and, in some cases,
support was missing. There are many combinations of things that mak
a failure to successfully sell. Marketing must do their research well an
depth to assure a solid market potential. You need to have an experie
marketing team that is willing to take the risk with you. Today enc
marketing information exists to make an intelligent and workable deci;
You should involve responsible salespeople that are aware of competi
As the CEO, you should call into account all of your key manager
people. Too often marketing is left out of this critical decision bec;
they are not a close part of the decision loop. Some management pe
do not understand the ability of good, focused, sales/marketing peopl
sniff out a market or potential. They know what will sell and to wh
They also are keenly aware of competition, to understand their streng
and weaknesses. They are the *bloodhounds* of good and proper research
the field. Without their inputs, management is operating in a vacuum a
will not meet a well-placed, comprehensive target.

With all of this incoming product information need, the ultim
decision maker needs to keep in mind those kinds of product that

their capability. It could happen that a very large, seemingly profitable requirement is uncovered, but it is very different from the family of ongoing products. The short life or difference of product could compromise the strong ability of the manufacturer to continue successful growth in the direction under way. The new idea could dilute efforts in a new direction away from the strength of this company. An example would be if a company is successful in building relays to customer's print. It is a labor-intensive business but profitable to this company. The new proposal is for a standard, low-cost relay that operates in run of the mill applications like washing machines. The per item profit is low; competition is fierce, and there is little customer loyalty. It would not support your overhead, which could be 400 percent, where custom work does support it. Don't be fooled by big, quick money. We almost did, but our chief turned it down. Again, your rep should understand your capability but send the opportunity in; we can always graciously turn it down.

Marketing Tool, DMS Register

If you are a US supplier of product to the military, you need to subscribe to DMS, Defense Marketing Services. This lists the DOD budget appropriations for government purchases of systems for ensuing years. This book shows the description of the system, the dollar amount of the contract, the number of systems, and the dollars to be paid each year for its contract life.

First you must determine if your product meets the controlling specification and if you are approved. Assuming that you are, you can then alert your salespeople to get involved with the government contractee to find out how many of your product are used per system and when. Let's say that XYZ Corporation has the contract for one thousand aircraft production per year starting in three years and running for ten years. Each aircraft uses fifty of your product at a price of $10 each. That equals $500 per plane times 10,000, which equals $5,000,000 total over ten years. If you're not approved and can be capable of being approved, have your salespeople get on it pronto. That big an order may prompt some expenditures on your part to improve product. Some value engineering will strengthen your position and improve the aircraft's performance. So, "Sell that!"

Enough Academics—Get to Work

Ed Bachorik must have been tired of seeing me in that office. We were growing so fast that we needed another outside sales rep to cover Northern New Jersey, and so he offered it to me. Without hesitation I gleefully accepted and made all kinds of rash promises on what he could expect from that territory. Rash quickly became real.

Ed said, "If you don't sell over there, don't come back here."

The Need Cries Out

So get off your butt and sell something! Commercial sales are elusive and different from the military. There are no known annual government budgets with central engineering and purchasing organizations. TAMs (total available market) must be determined by you as the sales manager, and the SAM (share of available market) inputs gotten from sales reps. A large segment of this market is hidden from popular view. It takes a concentrated, in-depth penetration by salespeople to identify it and to know how to apply your products into it.

As the salesperson in the field, you must learn all about your company's product capability and how it fits into a customer's application. You should get their specifications, read and understand them, and suggest a product that will suit. You may also offer available options that may be better than their specs require.

It is well for salespeople to perform this critical task, so decision makers on product availability are informed to meet established goals. No decision is more dependent on information than this sales input. So do it and be very accurate in doing so.

Keep in mind that basically your company is in the custom design and manufacturing business. No order, no manufacturing. Everything sold was a modification of a standard catalog item. Very little was built for stock.

Sales Lead and Pepsi

While selling OEM product as a salaried employee for Allied Control, I received this one suspicious-looking sales lead. It came from ads and inquiries as a response of a potential buyer. The office replied directly to the inquirer and gave the outside salesman, the rep, a copy to follow up on it. I almost threw this one away. I knew that the address was among multimillion-dollar homes in an elite area and not even close to mercantile establishments. However, I sought it out, and the place confirmed my doubts. It was a palatial home with an encircling blue stone gravel driveway. With boldness I drove up the driveway to the formidable entrance. I rang the chimes expecting to kill the lead. Apparently it was the butler who answered the door, and he directed me around back of the house on the blue stone gravel driveway. There appeared a very neat building with the man I had asked for, awaiting my arrival. He took me into his laboratory, which was very well equipped with electronic instruments. After thanking me for coming, he encouraged my effort by saying that he had a design contract from Pepsi Cola Corporation to update all of its dispensers nationwide. Could and would we help him in this design? We reviewed his specifications together and chose several of our products that would perform. How fast can I get to my boss to tell him about this, I thought! Later I delivered prototypes, and he tested them in his equipment. Subsequent modification discussions and meetings were held. This customer turned his new designs over to the manufacturer in another state. We alerted that rep covering the new account, and he got right on it. That is teamwork.

The outcome was that they used our product in the dispenser design. An out-of-town corporation manufactured the dispensers, giving us about $250,000 business. After that, every single lead was followed up with the effort to sell more product. Anyone going to the moon?

Hay Fever

We had just moved into a new home in Rockland County, New York, just north of New Jersey. My boss gave me those adjacent counties north of Jersey to cover. Most were a wilderness to us, but they were then mine to cover. Sales there were zero. One spring morning, suffering from hay fever and feeling like staying in, my conscience made me get ready to venture out—but where? Having this new, uncovered territory without one single lead or an idea where any potentials might be, I drove out toward a large city along the Ramapo Valley as my destination. Poking along US 17 near Sloatsburg, in the distance I saw a huge chimney but no smoke. Continuing on, I was reminded of the old smokestack selling technique, and here I was doing it! I went over the Ramapo River's wooden bridge and then up to a building at the base of the huge chimney, where I parked my shiny new Chevy. No horse to tie up! Inside of the International Fermont Corporation I asked for anyone who could help me. Mr. Al Levy came out and said that he was the chief engineer. Their product was standby diesel generators for airports, and they were bidding on an FAA contract to supply many of these systems. We discussed our products, and he chose several to be prototyped and used in the bid. Not knowing about Fermont, I thought it wise to follow through. I delivered the prototypes, and months later he called me to come and negotiate an order. We did, and he placed a multiyear contract for $100,000 a year. I should have hay fever more often!

American History

At National Fermont, the huge smokestack chimney was operating during the Revolutionary War with the British. It was used to draft a furnace that was smelting iron to make an immense anchor-like chain. The chain was anchored at West Point, to go through the Hudson River and then be fastened on the other end, at Cold Spring. It kept the British ships from passing. West Point has since become the famous United States Military Academy at West Point, New York. Smokestack selling still goes on! This is just an aside, but isn't it a great history lesson? Selling can be fun!

Keep On Keeping On

Al Levy of Fermont told me of a manufacturer north in Newburgh called Standard Winding Company. Still not feeling up to it, I found that company and its purchasing manager, Ken Van Wagner. There, Ken was charmed by my visit and pleased to have the attention of a salesman from New York City. It was like a wilderness; no rep ever ventured up there. We ate lunch at the landmark Beau Rivage Restaurant. Apologizing for not having a requirement for our product, Ken was happy to have made a new friendship, and I left our catalog and my card. Unbeknownst to either of us, a change was afoot at his company. They were bidding on the whole contract for which they previously only supplied transformers. Ken found our products listed, asked me to help him get them approved, and gave us a quarter million dollar order. Chalk up one great day of good fortune in selling!

Don't Call on Otis

Along the Hudson River in Yonkers is the massive Otis Elevator plant. I was told not to waste my time there because their product used components above our power handling capability. Because of its size, I was sure that they would use some of our products. The point, however, was that I was given the territory to cover, and cover it I did. I also needed to satisfy my curiosity about what went on there. The purchasing manager assured me that there was nothing there in elevator applications for us, *but* they had just purchased a small company named Bowl More, and they were looking for new products to apply and purchase. A few miles away I found that facility and introduced myself to Bob Webb, the chief engineer.

Accentuate the Positive

It seemed our competitor was approved with a style that we did not make. We, however, recently introduced another type of product not yet well known or even possibly not suited for this application of automatic bowling pinsetters. The possibility became real in my mind as a better idea for reliability, size, and cost. We could fit the function but were smaller than the form/fit. The potential use was thirteen units per machine. A powerful benefit was that our plant was only one and a half hours away so I personally took the specifications up there to engineering to see if we could supply relays for this lucrative application. In a week they replied and said we would mount our small relay in a plastic case that would mount in an octal plug arrangement. This design allowed service people to change out a unit by easy unplugging. The competition was in Chicago. Bob Webb allowed me to give him twenty-six prototypes, thirteen in each of two machines being tested. Ed Bachorik said to me, "Snyder, you're supposed to sell relays not give them away!" For months the tests continued, and I was there bowling with our relays doing the job. My average became 142! The day came when they asked me to be there at 2:00 p.m. on a Friday, and they would have a decision made as to which product would be used in the new pinsetters.

An Anxious Wait

My competitor left Webb's office, said hi to me, and left. Ushered in, I was questioned as to why my company was better than others, and I gave them plausible reasons why we were *the best*. I said that Allied Control was a family of 650 people, on the American Exchange, and we were number two in the commercial relay field. Our largest customer was their neighbor, IBM. This product is called the Volkswagen of the relay business. It's small, inexpensive, and very reliable. He asked me how big I thought their requirement was? Around $100,000, I guessed.

He flipped the order over in front of me, and the bottom line read $330,000. My eyes rushed to the top, and my company's name was on it. *Wow!* Being so elated, I expressed my thanks for his confidence and was sorry that we never even split a hot dog together.

"Too busy," he said.

"Well, how about celebrating our success," I said.

"How?" he asked?

"Well, let's get our wives and have dinner and see a Broadway play. That would be fun."

"What's a good play to see?" he asked.

"How about 'My Fair Lady,'" I said.

"What is that?" he asked.

I said, "It's the greatest musical of the times. You really have been too busy.

Bob Webb then said, "Sounds good, but sing something from it."

So I was singing "Wouldn't It Be Loverly," and in walks the president of the company, who laughingly said, "I've seen salesmen do all kinds of things to get an order. You're the first one to sing for his order."

I could not wait to buck the rush hour traffic to get to my boss in New York City, and I just made it. Breathlessly I told him about the decision and handed him the order, and he asked me if they had the money to pay for it.

"Owned by Otis Elevator," I muttered.

"Well I'll be a ---," he said, and grabbed his hat to take a bite. First time I was ever incorrigible with my boss, Ed.

Eventually, Bowl More had a grand opening and cocktail party at a new bowling alley in Larchmont. These new machines used many relays because the logic was then electronic rather than mechanical. Good for our relays! All of it was faster and better, with more options, and was less expensive.

Don't Go There!

Here I go again. DMS showed me that the parent company of our largest competitor, AMF, had received a contract to build launchers for the Saturn rocket program, so I went there, got the RFQ and made some good contacts in purchasing and engineering. Before that, at a sales meeting, my boss cautioned me not to waste time there because our competitor, being owned by AMF, would get the relay order. My boss was a prince and a joy to work for, but he did not know that our competitor did not make a military relay. He had confidence in me and trusted me. That's why I did what I thought was good business. The order covered our product and totaled $400,000 first release—my second incorrigibility to my boss, Ed.

What Happened to the Big Hitter?

These last two years were busy, a learning experience, rewarding, and a surprise. Not being in the office, I lost track of the company's sales figures. I assumed that Baltimore, Chicago, Dallas or Los Angeles reps were still the top reps. At our annual sales meeting, held atop the Essex House in Manhattan, our national sales team met for training and exposure to new products. At the conclusion, the first- and second-place sales awards were to be presented for two of these outfits. The loser was presented a knife by the winner to slit his throat. Second place was announced first. The runner-up award was given to our independent rep.

Ed Bachorik then paused to talk about "his misgiving at times for hiring this winner."

He also "wanted to kill him for being so stubborn."

"Most of all," he said, "this person was positively an inspiration to me."

"This rep brought in major business from new accounts."

Sitting in the back, I took all this in, wondering who Ed was talking about.

He said, "Stan Snyder, come up here; you're number one."

Along with a beautiful plaque, he also gave me the knife to be presented to the number two rep.

Being Incorrigible May Pay Off

A major company in New Jersey was the largest potential in dollars for my company's product in the Metro New York territory. It also was one of the largest in the country. Our company was approximately a 50/50 mix of commercial versus military products. Bendix Corporation's applications were for commercial airliners using military-approved product. Over the years we received only dribbles and drabs in business from Bendix. The products that they used were all military approved ones, of which we were approved and very competitive. I decided to penetrate this company by calling on all disciplines throughout the sprawling facility located next to Teeterboro Airport.

There were several reasons why we missed most of their business. Before my time, our sales coverage there was sporadic. Our competitor's rep was one of the best around and was a very sincere, likable guy. Each application required approval under stringent FAA requirements. Living there two days a week, I was attempting to establish a good image. Competition was in there tight and suffered no slipups that I knew about. One of the buyers and a component engineer and I clicked, and that was the beginning of success.

Doing It My Way for Ed

My boss noted that most of my expenses were entertaining people at this avionics company, and he said again, "Stop wasting time there." At that time my competitor rep told me to keep on because there were changes under way. At that point, we were approved on most major applications, which, if forecasted, would be a $3 million to $5 million a year business. That was the TAM for us at Bendix. This huge division of Bendix was called the Inertial Guidance Division. Imagination told me that these systems used many high-reliable relays, and we had the approved clean room manufacturing plant extension, just opened.

We Controlled ABC Network TV

We responded to an inquiry for many relays to be used in broadcasting "Cross Point and Tally Circuits. Our commercial relay model was very reliable, multicircuit, dust-covered, and inexpensive. Reliability was a factor because lost time on air is lost advertising revenue for ABC. After testing many types, ours was chosen, and we enjoyed that relationship for years.

Paperwork Failure

An account required our product to control a fire detection and exterminating system for Boeing's 727 aircraft. I recommended a miniature relay that had military approval. A dozen units were supplied to be life tested by the customer. After months of tests and evaluation, our relay was approved for that application, and a sources/specification was released to us to be quoted against and purchase orders placed. We supplied many thousands of relays against that specification, "Revision A." They were used without incident for several years.

Sometime later, I was called by the customer to recommend another product for the same application except the circuit load would then be 5 amps, instead of the ¼ amp for the ones previously supplied. These new units would be for the 727-300 stretch version aircraft, and heavier electrical loads were present in the new plane. After testing and approval, a "Revision B"_to the specification was made to cover this new relay.

Sometime later the customer called me to place a large order for thousands of the specification "Revision A," which notes I made in my Daytimer book, to be placed with the factory. Subsequently, the customer's confirming order was placed with us, which was compared to my verbal order and then released to our manufactory facility. These Rev A units were shipped and accepted by the customer; all well and good.

Lives Lost in Plane Crash!

Leaving LAX, a 727 aircraft fell from the dark sky over the Pacific Ocean. All aboard were lost. The black boxes indicated that the primary cause was the fire detection system, and our relays were in it. Further examination of the failed unit itself showed our relays had failed from an overload. Boeing Corporation located other planes produced around the time of the crashed one. They exhibited the same potentially deadly failure of the fire detection system, and our units were the cause. Customer, airline, and FAA officials converged on our company to precisely ascertain the cause and to pin the blame. I was interviewed as to my notes and how I verbally handled the order. The factory people were put on the spot as to how they handled the manufacture of the relays and how they were tested against the customer's order Revision A as ordered by the customer and relays accepted by them. They tested our relays to their Rev A spec, and they passed even when overstressed by a 100 percent overload.

These inquisitors returned to the customer's factory, where they found the problem that caused the failures. The application required Rev B relays, but their factory requisitioned Rev A units from purchasing. Purchasing placed Rev A. We built and shipped Rev A units, and the customer accepted Rev A.

Allied was formally absolved from blame. It gave me a greater respect for accounting and paperwork people, because this was a paperwork failure by our customer.

Our CEO, a Man of Integrity

After the dust settled down, and we all drew a deep sigh of relief, our CEO, Ed Gillette, called me in to discuss the tragedy and what he wanted me to do. He said to go over to the customer's plant and tell them that we would replace all of the misordered units for cost only. We took a hit for them, and it got us a great reputation all around.

Caught the Flying Bug

My best friend, Bob Larsen, took me flying in his Piper Cub two-seater aircraft from a small air park near home. I liked it so much that I decided to take lessons there to obtain a pilot's license. Needing extra cash, I signed up to sell Cutco Cutlery sets in the evenings. This excellent company, owned by Wearever Corporation, stressed intensive training. We needed to buy our own demo set to display to prospects. They did their homework so well that they determined that young, single, working girls living at home were prospects. They also knew that nurses and teachers were most likely to buy a set. Their training on an exact selling scheme demonstrating how each knife worked was recommended. Upon a successful sale, the total price was paid to me. I in turn paid a smaller sum to the company with the order. The difference between the selling price and the payment I made to the factory was about 30 percent. It was a nice margin, and I got paid before the factory. This arrangement is called a "distributor contract." I buy it and resell it. The company had strict rules of behavior and how we presented the product.

I made so much money in one year that it paid all of my training and was even enough to buy, with three others, a one-quarter interest in a brand new four-passenger Piper Cherokee 180D, fully equipped.

They enticed me to consider working full time, but my loyalty was to my boss Ed at Allied. This experience sharpened my wits to think standing up.

Upon one sales lead, I called at the home of a young lady and her mother. The demo went well and just before closing the dad walked in. Listening to my description of the knives material, the dad asked what the Rockwell Standard for hardness was. He was an engineer from Bendix. "I don't know, but I can find out," I said. I called my leader, Joe SataLucia, and he said "Scale H #40." The dad said, "That's great. Buy one set for mom and one set for daughter." And I thought that dad had killed my sale.

Only After-Hours Visits

I discovered a promising potential coming up with a major aircraft manufacturer in New Jersey. I was told that the R&D engineers that could see me for new products were up a hill in another building and could be visited only after 6:00 p.m. weekdays. This proprietary group was working on the very latest black box, which would record every function on the jet aircraft all the time it was running. They planned to use a dozen units in each box and planned three black boxes for each passenger jet. Engineers were looking for the smallest, two-pole sealed unit that would meet mil specs. We had just released our new miniature two pole, meeting all of the required mil specs. With many visits after six, the R&D engineers released our approval, and we received large orders as Boeing ordered black boxes. Subsequently, we know how completely these boxes have reported the status aboard an aircraft prior to a crash.

Good Things Come to Those Who Wait Upon

One day my big break came at Bendix! Our competitor dropped its rep firm, and my competitor friend was out, and I was the clown waiting in the wings. Purchasing became concerned over the rep change, so they asked my friend the product buyer to get someone else in the loop, and we were more than ready!

One stroke of creative selling got us in first place very quickly. While working with a project engineer on a brand new autopilot device for 727 aircraft that required many of our relays, I wondered if he had ever flown as a pilot where their products were used. He said no. I asked him out to a brown-bag lunch the next day. I flew in our new Piper Cherokee and parked it next to the plant. I took him up for lunch, and he got the hands-on experience of using the type of product that he designed, which my plane had. Back on the ground, we discussed a new relay that we just released as smaller, faster, more reliable, and less expensive. Our first big order from Bendix came from that effort. When he got over getting that first large order from Bendix, my boss then wondered if I carried enough insurance on that plane to cover a happening to a customer. "How about one million dollars a passenger seat?" I assured him.

This account continued to place the forecasted volume of business, which was in the millions. This was the third time I was incorrigible, and it paid off! In the field, you are the P&L manager! It's your territory, and your butt that's on the line.

More Fun in the Air

My close friend Bob Larsen said that an inventor friend started a company in a building at Teeterboro Airport next to Bendix. There I found Allen Heinsohn working on a new angle of attack system for aircraft. This new invention gave the pilot a reading to control the aircraft while flying. It was a more accurate way of knowing how to pilot more precisely with much greater safety than by using only an airspeed indicator. This device, approved by the FAA for certain aircraft, was being produced by Heinsohn's company, the Monitair Corporation. Each unit required several relays that were very similar to the ones used by Bendix. Our relays were used to interconnect the black box to a sensor, warning lights, horn, and the autopilot. We enjoyed a modest amount of business from Monitair, and I was proud of helping Heinsohn's success. As a new pilot, Heinsohn used me to study my performance using this unique new device. I've done many things to write business, but this was the most fun of all. Al owned a fast Piper Twin Comanche, which he used to test my ability to learn flying it. While I controlled the aircraft, we made five touch-and-go runs while I used the angle of attack instrument to read lift. On the last run over a factory at the edge of the airport, Allen asked me how fast I thought we were going. "Must be about 80 mph," I said. He uncovered the airspeed indicator, and it actually was 60 mph, and I almost wet my pants because I thought it was dangerously too slow. The new instrument measures lift, which was ample. We continued our relationship for years.

Another Reported Failure

It seems that too many Lear Jets began to lose control while on final approach to landing. The autopilot systems caused the planes to dive until the pilots rescued the aircraft from crashing. The erroneous signal was caused by a relay, which had apparently failed in that mode. I was called to their lab to witness the engineer breaking open our relay to determine the cause of failure. I would not permit them to do this until one of our engineers could be present. Two hours later our chief engineer arrived to peel open the sealed relay to find nothing amiss. Others were opened to exhibit the same excellent appearance as they had so performed before opening. We left in a quandary, not knowing how to help them. It was later determined by the customer that harnessing inside of the air column was too taut, which caused a short in the relay circuit. There was another great sigh of relief from all of us who were involved.

This Time We Did Fail

On another Friday we got a call that an Air Force One 707 jet was put on hold because of a failure. We got the relay untouched, and everyone in need watched as it was peeled open. To our dismay, a solder ball got loose inside and shorted out two circuits. We had discontinued this relay some time ago because of solder contamination problems. A new, welded relay was given to replace it. We never knew what the application was. We only knew that President Johnson was delayed because of it.

A New Challenge

Allied was growing fast, and loyal, capable people were being moved up. They promoted me to field sales manager, to be responsible for our independent rep network and the development of sales. I don't know how capable I was, however. It seemed easier to work alone, but now I had the opportunity to encourage, support, and inspire our reps. Was this selling, I wondered? Experience then taught me that it was selling of the highest order. I instructed the field reps about new products and described unique applications that I had seen. Then I helped them apply it in landing new business for us. There was occasion to offer these men a special incentive to get a new program moving that would net some profitable business. Supporting these successful reps to write new business was key to our success and also was a new learning curve for me.

The incentives between them and me were different. Believe it or not, my main reason to be successful out in the field was to please my boss. In so doing he took care of all that I needed and wanted. As a company man, my loyalty and pride of product spurred me on to success. Pay was important but not primary in my case.

On the other hand, our reps were driven by commission, not loyalty to us or primarily pride in product. Within their own organization, the motives may be the same. The key to good sales management, I think, is the ability to work well with salespeople to help their success by praise when they need it. A manager must find joy in seeing his people attain their own level of success. This nationwide network of experienced salespeople can do wonders for your effort toward a common goal. Is this selling? You bet it is, and I love it!

Listen to the Crying

Now that all of these turned-on people are out there beating the bushes, they often come back with requirements for product that we do not make. Not understanding, they would say, why not? This set me to thinking. Why not be creative in our forecasting effort. Periodically we asked our reps to forecast what business they saw coming in the next period. Invariably they would forecast for-sure business based on history. These conservative, for-sure documents were helpful for manufacturing only. There were no new targets to be addressed or increases in volume for marketing to appraise. Naturally the reps were careful not to list an unsure item, where they could be criticized if it was missed. I assured them that if they gave us a comprehensive listing with a probability percentage on each item, we would respond accordingly. What I wanted was a listing of all products of our category listed with application info, quantity, price, schedule, competition, and length of use or product life. What we got was a huge list of products called TAM. This marketing tool gave us insight for new products because now our reps became dreamers, which caused us to be creators of new products! I sold them on the company and on our response capability; they in turn sold the customer. The old way of forecasting was set up by accounting minded people and would not inspire new business.

Max-imize Sales

You've got to love the traveling around and working with new individuals. On one such trip, I met a new man working for our rep. Max took me off into an unknown territory. He reminded me of my hay fever and the first time out selling in that new territory. Max had a good contact at an elevator company out in the boondocks. They purchased product way above our power-handling capability. Max knew this but said they buy coils to assemble into another product. A coil being a part of our relays, we only paid a 2 percent commission. Max said that they buy hundreds of thousands of these coils and would we consider raising the commission rate. "Get me the specs, and I think I can get you the increase," I said. We raised the commission to 5 percent, quoted the one hundred thousand coils, and Max placed the order for one hundred thousand. That order, which amounted to $250,000, was profitable for us and the rep. Negativeness doesn't sell product! Some months later, on my next trip back there, I presented the commission check to Max's boss, Bob Infanger, who was greatly pleased with Max. He then gave Max a nice bonus check. I love it! He sold; I sold. He sold—all sold. We Max-imized effort.

A Hunting Trip

Our largest account, AT&T Western Electric, had factories in North Carolina. Being a house account and our largest customer, it was the only business coming from that area. Knowing the account fairly well, I was unsure of any new business that we could have. Being handled remotely, we were really not penetrated there. Changes in the Bell System removed our inside G2 from corporate, so we operated in a vacuum Also, being on the toad, I was no longer close to the account. Since my longtime friend Clyde Dula was working for a rep, I asked him if he could cover that territory. Sorry, he said that he represented a competitor there. Now I knew we had better have an outstanding rep in that territory. I interviewed all around that territory and could not find an interested rep because they knew the major bucks coming out of the territory were for a no-commission house account. At Western Electric a buyer friend told me about a former employee who had just set up his own new rep company. Phil Nahser, an engineer from WE, convinced me to consider his selling for us. We talked together and dreamed a little, but he was not interested in pioneering a desolate territory for us at zero percent commission from an account that he knew thoroughly. Knowing the account, I convinced our management to allow the full 5 percent for new product purchases developed there. I returned to hire Phil and to work with him. He produced a fair amount of new business from new accounts, and he set up several distributors there.

Phil Makes It *Big*!

The day arrived when Phil put me to the task. He knew of a bid that would be due in several months to be bought by WE in great volume. He had the specs, and it was for a product close to our design mechanically but a perfect match for our electronic capability. Our application people said it's not our footprint and not mil approved. The volume was large enough for me to refuse a no quote and to take it to our VP engineering for him to reply. The first quantity was ten thousand units at last purchase price obtained by Phil of $52 each. That's a lot of money to move on, so the VP came up with a design and gave it to our costing group to quote. They were not given competition's price of $52 each, which gave great encouragement to take a risk. They officially gave me $17.34 each as a fair and reasonable price. Knowing Nahser's info on competition's last price, we could trust what Phil told us. Cost accounting officially gave me a $17.34 price. There remained only a short time to build prototypes and submit them to Bell Laboratories for approval before the North Carolina Works could purchase the relays. Because of our near-perfect record with the Bell System, they accepted our protos and expedited approval via me because of my longtime friendship. The director at Bell called the buyer and verbally released the Allied approval. Knowing this, my friend Phil, the rep, bugged me for the price due for the bid in a week. I asked Phil to give me the price that he thought would get the order from the closed bid opening the next Monday at 2:00 p.m. Every day Phil asked, and I replied for him to tell me. Knowing the value of this potential business, I trusted in Phil's judgment. He bugged me all the way to early Saturday evening, when he called me at home and once more implored me to give him the price. "Phil, calm down, have a drink, make a guesstimate, and call me back," I said. Later Phil called and said to give him authority to quote $50.25 each, delivery to meet or exceed customer's requirement. "Please, Stan, don't fire me if we miss! Be sure to call me after the bid opens," I requested.

At 3:00 pm that Monday, Phil called and excitedly yelled, "We were low bidder!" Competition surely was asleep at the switch, I thought.

The profit between $50.25 and the cost of $17.34 is a whopping $33.00 a unit times ten thousand pieces, or a total of $330,000.00 pure profit, not to mention the normal profit in the $17.34 cost price.

The lessons learned here are multiple:

- First, choose a rep who understands the product as it applies to his identified market TAM. Choose one who has a passion to be involved and to sell—one who is not afraid to take risks to land good, profitable business.

- My good and trusting friendships with the key people in the Bell System for over two decades produced excellence for them at good prices, and this partnership gave Allied Control millions of dollars of business during and after that period.

- Be able to work closely with your inside people until they say no, can't do it.

- Then consort with the decision makers to affect the offering of a new and promising potential.

In Memory of Charles Schneider

When Charley retired, he was director of switching apparatus for the Bell Laboratories. He was a highly respected electrical engineer who demanded compliance to specifications that he wrote and who was the manager of programs under his aegis. We enjoyed traveling together, and I took directions from him to communicate his way of excellence to my people at Allied. Because of his trust in our company, he took a risk to approve what turned out to be a superior product and made me very proud of our relationship.

I believe Charley passed away in the 1970s. There was no one to replace him, at least in my way of thinking.

"Welcome to the Conglomerate—You're Fired!"

That was the title of a book written by Arthur Hailey and is appropriate to this startling situation.

Allied Control was sold to a company that had a history of taking over companies and later divesting them of their saleable assets. Before this could happen, they lobotomized the company of its management people with know-how who were an intimate part of its success. After twenty wonderful years at Allied, they let me go with severance pay. To me it was like getting kicked out of my family. It was because we were an intimate group of folks working together toward success in the company. Later I learned that the Bell System pulled Allied's approval on major military business managed by them. Where did all of that business go? Most of it went to competitors. It was a little like digging a hole at the edge of the sea. As long as you kept digging, the work was viable. Stop and the sea took over like a flood of competition.

Heading South

Allied's rep in Florida made the most interesting offer for me to sell components in the Tampa Bay area. I knew that Florida, formerly 7 percent of the national electronics market, was growing rapidly, so the challenge was mine. There were several offers of positions around the country to again use my experience to participate in helping it grow. During those five years, I learned a lot about component sales of many different products. That rep companies sold for first-rate companies such as Grayhill, Sealectro, McGill, Allied, and Varo.

Grayhill—Of Great Integrity

Grayhill was founded and directed by Ralph Hill, who had experience as a rep. They design and manufacture the finest rotary switches in the world. At the time, Bruce Vinkmulder was their marketing director. Big Bruce, a big man, was an even bigger inspiration to salesmen like me. Bruce would say, "Go thou forth and sell," which I did as first priority. They also were very generous with commission payments—more than any other principals we had. Grayhill also had a *Red Book*, which was their engineering bible for switch applications.

Very early one morning, Ralph Hill called me to ask if I was the one who sold a special military-approved switch to E Systems there in St. Petersburg. "Yes," I replied. "Why?"

He said, "We may have omitted a vital antivibration part in the units shipped to them. I want you to go to the customer's plant to determine if they are missing the part and how many."

I said, "Ralph, you're opening Pandora's box. Are you sure?"

"----? I'm not asking you. I'm telling you to go and see."

I did, immediately.

The AVS part was missing from units in receiving, on the line, and in completed shippable systems. The rest were in an airborne application.

By noon I reported the news that his suspicions were correct, and a steady stream of those units were promptly returned, and each of thousands were repaired and returned within twenty-four hours at no out-of-pocket cost to E Systems. The customer was very impressed with Grayhill's forthright handling before the customer realized there would be a major problem later in the aircraft application.

Part of good selling is a trusting relationship with the manufacturer and rep. When a problem occurs, and they do, we are rated by how quickly we respond to solve the issue. It is a valuable selling tool! Again, I call it "response capability." As a result, I sold thousands more of Grayhill product to E Systems because we proved our worth. As the rep, I was a chauffeur for these switches back and forth from the airport. Being a servant is a blessing to those we represent and our customers.

That kind of rare integrity turned me on to sell more Grayhill wherever I could. They are the best!

Square Pegs in Round Holes

My friendship with Allied's Dallas rep, Preston Ammon, gave me a great opportunity to sell a unique new product that could vastly change the interconnect methods used by firms building systems requiring a way of interconnecting a mother board of ten thousand pins. Very expensive wire wrap machines were used to accomplish that many connections reliably. Preston's newly acquired firm, Elfab Corporation, was the base for him to invent a system now known as press-fit technology. We all knew that soldered connections were faulty where extremely low levels of signals were handled. Wire wrap required large, expensive machines to be used. His invention utilized multilayer PC boards with as many as ten boards, with a total of twenty insulated circuits. Via holes were drilled into the ten boards. These holes were plated to accept the square press-fit pins. By the ability to create software developed from the two from list, this system became a logic board. The press-fit pins were then to pick up or pass deeply buried circuits in the system.

The daughter board side ends of the inserted pins were stamped out to be inserted into a plastic connector accepting the daughter cards or memory cards. Not one drop of solder was used anywhere in this system because each individual pin was designed to have an extraction force from a single PCB of fifteen pounds each. That's phenomenal!!

Grasping the immense potential of this press-fit technology, I obtained the line from Preston for our rep firm to sell it in Florida.

Is This Too Technical to Grasp?

My selling this product to engineers was pure joy because it was new and unique. One after another were sold this device. It was fun negotiating the orders with the buyers because I let them take the credit for discovering this new product. At our largest user, the company canceled several millions of dollars of wire wrap systems obsoleted by the new press-fit technology, solderless backplanes.

The rep firm I worked for did not grasp the potential for this product, nor were they in-depth enough to sell it to major users. Eventually I left that firm to join up with a small firm that offered opportunity for me to be more than just a salaried salesman.

The Elfab Corporation account decided to follow me in this new venture, and I was able to quickly develop $3.5 million in sales by traveling around the state of Florida. At 5 percent commission, which amounts to $175,000, that was quite a disparity to my salary of $40,000 a year with no other perks.

Going It Alone Again

With the encouragement of several of our best principal suppliers, I left that rep firm, which had grown from one man to six men since I started there. Their total annual sales were $5 mil, of which I brought in $3.5 mil.

I started my own rep firm with loans and my own capital and with huge encouragement from my wife, Judy, who was made secretary/treasurer of Trimark Associates Inc.

The name Trimark means there are three elements to our marketing setup. They are: the customer, the supplier, and me. Our logo was a simple triangle. As an aside, for some it stands for the Trinity.

Our base line or product was Elfab and their new press-fit backplane. We quickly added EBM miniature fans, Allied Control relays, NCR power supplies, and KIP Inc. transformers and valves. Also, we were seeking a few compatible others.

A call from Preston of Elfab gave me another large challenge. Preston purchased a fledgling, functional board-level test system, way beyond my scope of product knowledge. This company, called Scientific Machines Co., had a group of software engineers with a small production facility in Dallas near Elfab. Not one customer was in Florida.

Functional testers were new to me and didn't fit our component sales compatibility. In deference to my friendship with Preston and his pressure for me to sell the testers, I relented. We agreed that my main effort would be with Elfab's backplane customers, with the exception of the military accounts. After being trained and given a demo system, I went forth to sell. These units operated under "Unix" software with an innovative method of testing computer circuits. The testers had an onboard fault combination library in them, and faults were put into the circuits looking for a match. This detection method was thorough and had a detection ratio as high as 92 percent. A customer could secretly open or short the node, and the machine could detect an open or a short there in seconds. This feature astounded the engineers, because prior to that one needed to isolate the node by hand to test it. Aren't I smart to know all of this without being an engineer! I still sell the sizzle its uniqueness, cost advantage, and me for support.

Their sales manager, Randy, wanted me to establish a priority list of the most likely accounts for us to visit together. To do this, one must first determine the market—what is needed when, how many, and what are the designer's wishes. It's always good to have a good friend in high places. All of these parameters were in place when my priority list of accounts to be sold showed that E Systems was bidding a huge contract where 10 percent of the contract would be for test systems to assure their reliability. My friend urged me to get in there pronto, which we did on the next Monday. Three complete demos later, they asked us to come back after lunch, when we performed other demos for more engineers. On Tuesday, we did our demo before an audience of various disciplines. That afternoon they asked us to quote test systems and simulators. The simulators, which SMC also designed and built, were to be used by the customers to write for themselves the software to run the tests.

The specs were turned over to us for SMC, and we again were urged to quote by Thursday latest. My people crunched and cranked out an offer to sell. That offer quote was a book. I delivered the quote on Thursday, and the customer put our proposal into their bid the next day. Our offer was over $5,000,000 first release. I asked the SMC engineer and Preston if we could handle it, since that dollar amount equaled the new test company's annual sales. Preston had access to hefty banking support, and I knew personally that he would never let a good customer down.

Several weeks later they got the contract, and we were awarded the order for simulators and testers. Our commission on first release was a whopping 13 percent, the balance at 10 percent!

To sell an extremely involved technical product to people you're not familiar with requires being a little crazy in the first place. To do it for a friend and to protect your contract with him to sell backplane business is good sense. To choose the right priority account and to seek the right help to present the product to engineering management is composite wisdom, which comes from experience. To write a multimillion dollar contract out from under the big test system outfits takes chutzpah. I wasn't familiar to their reps, so they didn't perceive the threat. When calling on E-Systems, I signed in as the rep for Elfab, which meant backplanes, not test equipment. Once I learned about and believed in the product's special features, I could boldly sell that feature, knowing it offered much greater value. The KG84 contract lasted for years, and we continued to enjoy future releases.

Remember, E Systems was the account that Grayhill Switch rescued from its error. Same company, same people!

Fired Again

This time it was NCR that fired all of their independent reps because the corporation's GP (gross profit) was below target, and it was an easy fix to add our 5 percent commission to the bottom line. Subsequently they lost all of their key accounts in our territory. Our key account with them was the Paradyne Corporation, and we missed that income from selling NCR power supplies. We were their largest power supply rep in the United States.

Out of the blue came a Dr. Stan Hahn, from Moraga California, who was looking for a good rep to sell custom power supplies to his first major OEM. In dollar contrast to the now lost income from NCR, it would be an uphill, tough battle, because they had no image to build on. I really liked this well-spoken Korean man. His EE degree was from NYU, and Stan wound up in California, where he was awarded a doctor of computer science degree. He and his wife, Alice, established AMS Corporation to design product, contract its manufacture in Korea, and manage it. Before his first trip with me to Paradyne, and to assure that he could meet or exceed NCR's power supply business, I explained in depth a time line required to get approved on a single product. If he was willing, could meet their requirements, and be competitive, the risk then was time and possibly not getting the business after many months of effort. After all, I had seen my competitors suffer this.

Paradyne is eminently fair, and they encourage a partnering effort. Stan came in on our second visit with a prototype that knocked their socks off. It was much smaller, faster, and better, had more options, met all safety issues, and was less expensive. This unique product would be made abroad under AMS strict control. This power supply was sold for an unheard of time of ten years in their equipment. Stan had the capability to design, manufacture, and deliver, but he was lacking account knowledge or how to meet a time line schedule. We knew our accounts in depth. Our partnership produced good results for the three of us.

A second application arose for us to replace the NCR unit in a new server design. An NCR unit was large and heavy, and Stan designed a more powerful, faster, smaller, and lighter unit Its cost was appreciably lower. At the beta site demo, for approval of their customer, we faced what I call a "tip-tivity" test. With the lighter power supply they installed, they needed to widen the footprint of the standing cabinet. The heavier NCR supply added weight at a low center of gravity at the bottom of the cabinet. Ours was simply too light. We all live and learn, but AMS continued to be a good supplier to Paradyne.

One of Paradyne's engineers was working on a business degree, and he used the wisdom of Stan Hahn in organizing AMS and its success.

Partnering

I sold for millionaires' companies with great experience, and they were respected by me. Now practicing their profession, I constantly felt the need to learn more to better handle our customer needs. One such opportunity offered great wisdom, and I later preached it. As Joe Girard wrote, "The dealings between buyer and seller are mainly adversarial." I have been aware of this at times, but I tried not to join in that kind of behavior. Joe, of course, was successful in selling autos! In fact, he sold more than any one single person by being creative and by using unique proactive methods to sell autos.

Cost of Ownership

What is cost of ownership? This very thorough method gives the buyer the realistic reason to purchase a product, not just a price. It puts numbers to historical performance of a supplier and eliminates a cheap device from blowing up and killing people. (Remember the cheap connecter in Apollo 13.) First of all, the buyer does not see a bid or quote until it is run through his company's computer system for a rating. Here's an example: along with our competitors, we are asked to quote ten thousand of a certain product that at that quantity normally would cost $10 from each of three companies. The computer would give company A the $10.00 buy price. Company B was given a buy price of $10.15. Our companies computed price, that the buyer saw, was $9.75, to pay us actually the $10.00 cost we needed. Our performance rating over time was excellent, thus our loaded price showed up at $9.75 for that buy, but the computer paid us $10.00. The other two companies didn't have as good of a history, consequently their prices were $10.00 and $10.50. These became the magic numbers that the buyer used to guide his buy decision. This program was taught and managed by Collins Radio-Rockwell. They design and build avionic systems for commercial aircraft.

Paradyne practiced a similar program entitled "Partnering." If the incumbent supplier performed well, kept his cost down and offered assistance in bettering product, and responded well to complaints, they were a good partner and had the inside track on any new business. As the rep for two suppliers that enjoyed being a partner of the Paradyne

Corporation, I was honored to be an ex officio member of their product management team having to do with our product. I had no authority there, but my inputs were valued, and their comments were reported and taken seriously by my principals. A failure offers opportunity to prove our ability to respond appropriately. I call that "response capability." They didn't beat us into submission when something went wrong. Paradyne hosted an annual "suppliers' day conference," where everyone listened up for what was going to happen. This company treated us reps like royalty, and it got the company very positive results and loyalty!

Selfishly, when my retirement was due, I thought it should be at Paradyne, where my history and loyalty to many friends remains.

Managing Your Representative

I believe in contracting individual rep companies that have been successful in selling similar products, especially if they were successful in selling your product. In my case, that would have been relays. They must be targeting markets with key accounts that purchase components. There are some exceptions, such as the power supply, which itself is a system, but most applications make it a component to power a larger system. It is necessary to know and understand what kinds of systems companies buy large quantities of your product. Components include relays, transformers, connectors, resistors, wire, PCBs, and all manner of semiconductors.

It is well to visit key accounts around the country with your rep. Encourage him to plan the visit to be in-depth, in order for you to assess his expertise and how you may best support his efforts there.

Consider having several key people from major potential outfits, working in purchasing, sales, and engineering, to be a part of your marketing information team. These would be people interested in giving you information about what their company could use in future applications. This form of partnering can benefit you and the customer, to be up to date on designs by using the expertise of both companies for mutual benefit. Each such arrangement may be customized to suit the situation and hopes of each company. Mutual trust is necessary. Your good, supportive management is key to the success expected.

Following the 80/20 law, (80 percent of business comes from 20 percent of companies) visit those potentials with your rep.

On these territorial visits, make attempts to include each salesperson on the team. Even an unlikely person, if interested, can do good for you by being recognized as needed. Consider Max in the Max-imize story related earlier. Your selling technique can be employed with such a person.

Inside personnel of the rep's office may be included in a general product training meeting, which you should hold periodically. Don't wait for reps to attend your annual sales meeting. Hold a pizza party to talk about how valuable inside people can be for your effort.

Hidden Potentials

While working with the sales correspondents of your company and the sales for the month look dim, the potential is close at hand. Go to the office of each sales correspondent to review open quotations. I'll bet you that there are sizable quotes just awaiting a response from the rep about that potential. Have the correspondent call the rep to request a report on status of the quote. Follow that up and respond accordingly.

One time doing this, I found a large quote made to a company in the middle of Alabama. The rep responded to say that their bid looked good, and we *may* get the order. This $100,000 potential was too good to say we *may* get the order. The next day, the rep and I drove to the potential with a lunch date in mind with the buyer. We offered a better savings by giving them a 2 percent thirty-day payment term, and the buyer was pleased. They gave us a tour of their facility, and we could see potentials for other products. We received that order and others like it to make our bookings over the top. Sometimes, the gold mine is our own sales files.

Lost-Business Reports

Ouch, but why do people want to hide these? A lot can be learned from them by getting involved to know why and then hopefully correct the problem. What did the rep have to say? Did we query the buyer? Was our price too high, late delivery, not rep connected, poor image, or simply not approved by the customer. See the problem? Do something to improve it. A customer never really knows how good you are until you have a problem, and you solve it to his benefit. By listening to what he wants and trying your best to apply, it is good business in deed.

Intelligent Forecasting

Once a year we requested our sales and rep teams to forecast new business for the upcoming year. What they turned in was a very weak help.

They stated the current year plus a 5 percent increase. A little like GNP growth. We learned little from these, which was not very inspiring to anyone in our system. Having the DMS register, we knew what military budgets were funded, and what companies got the contracts. We also knew how many systems were contracted over what period of time. A good rep should be able to report how many of our product would be purchased by that customer. Continued follow-up by your rep is necessary to assure success. He is then able to forecast with an intelligent probability. I like 95 percent for us! A large potential with a low probability on forecast requires you to hop on it by visiting the customer with the rep.

On the commercial side, it required an organized system of new product ideas and information. Our reps were requested to list potentials known by them and to give us type, quantity, required delivery over time, and target price. Getting with the right people in the customer's facility and listening with an open mind can bring about new products and ideas. Are approved potentials out there where we are not approved, and can we be approved?

Composing a list of a customer's target challenges and then presenting it to listening ears at your company can bring about improvements and possibly new products. Your rep is key to progress and success!

Selling to Your Own Company

Some of these new ideas/products have caused great interest in your company's management. Again, a good, knowing rep can be pivotal in encouraging you and your company to consider taking a risk to develop a new commercial product. You can, with the backing of your rep, eventually give to the board of directors reasons why it would be a good risk to invest on a large scale to tool and produce a new product. Through your rep teams around the country you know that, according to their forecasts, there is a large ongoing potential, ongoing base for this type of device. It may even be a breakthrough in the market. Keep in mind the 80/20 law, and be comprehensive in your report.

You, as the sales manager, are responsible for composing this list of known application and its potential to the board of directors for their decision. If you did your homework well and rechecked the potentials, which is mandatory, and this proposal of new business is broad-based, you then have confidence to present it to the board for action.

This entire effort can be called "response capability."

Where do completely new products come from? These are totally new to the field. The need is yet unfilled by any known proposal. It's not a form, fit, and functions substitute. Why, it must be our R&D engineering. True, but where did they get the idea from? It came from a customer's need through the rep or sales to the management of our company. These questions need to be understood and posed to get the information to enable us to make a good business decision. Let's assume that it's a relay, although other components would fit the same assessment. Here they are:

Quantity to be used over what period of time?

A well-known, stable company has an application for something that will switch at nanosecond speeds. Nothing mechanical can perform this fast. Research has shown that the potential will be mind-boggling.

No one, however, has yet offered a product, as far as we know. If we have the capitol and effort to risk, we could become a leader in the field. A large part of that decision is how strong are our reps? Are they willing to risk their assets to help?

If we think they are, and we include them in our decision circle, we could offer larger commissions to help. With imaginative plans, we could also make area reps into our regional managers, under a custom plan. At least they should be brought into our intelligence network. This is what we need to know:

circuit or application parameters

operating voltage

contact arrangement

applied loads at what voltage

hermetically sealed, dust cover, or open type

life expectancy at full loads

safety issues, e.g., UL, VDE, CSA

product proposed

rate of delivery

target price

number of first article prototypes needed and by when

levels of customer's management that will be involved

new final application parameters (to design an entirely new product just for them, which may be proprietary to them if they pay some of the tooling costs)

rep's guesstimate of percentage of order placed by a certain date (such as, 80 percent sure by June first of this year)

None of this potential could happen without a turned-on rep. When I was selling direct for my company, I uncovered a huge number of product going to a single competitor for a bowling machine pinsetter application. It was the first machine to be offered to bowling alleys that utilized electrical logic, replacing mechanical logic that sequentially operated machines. Therefore, smaller, faster, multicircuit units were sought by customer. We studied the specifications and supplied a much smaller unit, at higher speed, requiring less power, and costing less. Ultimate life was an order of magnitude better. {10 million cycles Min.}

I gave them twenty-six prototypes for testing, and we were awarded the order for $230,000 first release units, some months later. The time line was twelve weeks.

Dream on and dream away; it will pay you one day!

Suggested Time Line Development Schedule:

March 1— Rep locates potential and obtains specifications.

March 10—Rep delivers a quotation with options of quantity and design.

March 30—Customer responds with order for prototypes to be evaluated.

April 15—Rep delivers protos.

May 1—Customer requests modifications on protos.

May 10—Rep delivers mods and reviews spec change at no more cost.

May 10—Customer runs final units in machines for compliance.

May 25—Units pass tests in system.

May25—Rep orders safety tests started, UL and CSA

July 1— Rep informs customer that units are safety listed.

July 15—Customer advises that we are approved to revised specification.

Rep is patient!

August 1—Customer advises rep to negotiate final production order for 20,000 units. (He's been camping in the customer's parking lot.)

August 1—Customer places final order with delivery schedule.

Rep joyfully follows up this order until complete. Next order?

In Conclusion

Some folks think that a good salesman is a macho guy who is pushy and aggressive. Joe Girard writes in his book *The Greatest Salesman on Earth* that the relationship between buyer and seller is "adversarial." At the time Joe sold more automobiles than any other person. He was that successful by being creative and persistent in reaching his goal. His idea of adversarial practices has been often practiced even in my area of selling. Not having products or services to sell that you believe in may require that kind of selling or trickery practices. Joe sold so many new cars because of his wit and persistence. Joe also offered great advice to prospective salespeople, such as, "Don't join the coffee klatch." His advice was clear that we should not get involved with Monday morning quarterbacking, because it spews out negativity. Even my friend and leader Ed Bachorik was at times negative about certain potential prospects, which I later proved to be a big success in writing large amounts of business. He was right that he put me out there to sell, and being out there I knew the potentials well. One thing is sure. I never let Ed down, because he trusted me to do a good job. To please him was a major motive in my success.

Creative Selling—What Is It?

I've heard of this, but what is it? How can we create a need? A market is created by need. After all of these great, exciting experiences along this wonderful journey, what can I say? I think I got it!

Assemble a team of good salespeople to sell an exciting, creative idea/product. Go into the North Pole marketplace and make this pitch:

We have an excellent product that you need here. This product is inexpensive—practically no cost to operate—will never wear out, is attractive, and delivery is immediate. Our warranty is the best, and you certainly need this product. What is it man? *Refrigerators!* What on earth could they be for up here in the cold, where only Eskimos live?

It will keep their food from freezing. Right! How many, please?

Now Retired?

Greatest Joy of All!—Is It Selling?

Late in my life, I learned that each of us is endowed with special abilities or spiritual gifts. If we use them as we are created to do, we can then achieve personal success. I believe that I am fortunate to have followed my abilities or gifts, even though early on I was not aware of them as such. Hopefully, your passion is in line with your gifts. I firmly believe that an average person, who is young at heart and is driven by the possibility of success in the selling field, should go for it. The rewards are great!

God called me at age sixty-nine to be ordained a deacon.

In this ministry, I serve the Lord through his people. I'm not selling, just giving, and that is pure joy!

Stanley B. Snyder

trimark7@verizon.net